DECOMPOSERS
Worms

by Trudy Becker

FOCUS READERS®
BEACON

www.focusreaders.com

Copyright © 2025 by Focus Readers®, Mendota Heights, MN 55120. All rights reserved. No part of this book may be reproduced or utilized in any form or by any means without written permission from the publisher.

Focus Readers is distributed by North Star Editions:
sales@northstareditions.com | 888-417-0195

Produced for Focus Readers by Red Line Editorial.

Photographs ©: iStockphoto, cover, 1, 4, 10, 14, 25; Shutterstock Images, 6, 8, 17, 19, 22, 27, 29; Ariadne Van Zandbergen/Alamy, 12; Paul R. Sterry/Nature Photographers Ltd/Alamy, 21

Library of Congress Cataloging-in-Publication Data
Names: Becker, Trudy, author.
Title: Worms / Trudy Becker.
Description: Mendota Heights, MN: Focus Readers, 2025. | Series: Decomposers | Includes index. | Audience: Grades 2-3
Identifiers: LCCN 2024035347 (print) | LCCN 2024035348 (ebook) | ISBN 9798889984023 (hardcover) | ISBN 9798889984306 (paperback) | ISBN 9798889984849 (pdf) | ISBN 9798889984580 (ebook)
Subjects: LCSH: Worms--Juvenile literature.
Classification: LCC QL386.6 .B43 2025 (print) | LCC QL386.6 (ebook) | DDC 592/.3--dc23/eng/20240830
LC record available at https://lccn.loc.gov/2024035347
LC ebook record available at https://lccn.loc.gov/2024035348

Printed in the United States of America
Mankato, MN
012025

About the Author

Trudy Becker lives in Minneapolis, Minnesota. She likes exploring new places and loves anything involving books.

Table of Contents

CHAPTER 1
Dirt for Dinner 5

CHAPTER 2
How They Decompose 9

CHAPTER 3
Helping the Ecosystem 15

THAT'S AMAZING!
Worms and Water 20

CHAPTER 4
Worm Danger 23

Focus Questions • 28
Glossary • 30
To Learn More • 31
Index • 32

CHAPTER 1
Dirt for Dinner

A worm moves slowly through the damp dirt. It **contracts** its slimy body. Then the worm slides forward again. It is time to eat. The worm reaches a dense patch of soil. It opens its mouth wide.

The mucus on a worm's body helps it breathe. Mucus also helps the worm move through dirt easily.

> Worms don't have eyes. They use things such as light, heat, and smells to find their way.

Then it keeps pushing ahead. The worm's lip helps collect the dirt. The soil goes straight into its mouth. Then the worm's throat grabs the soil. The worm swallows its meal.

But the worm is not done eating yet. It smells pieces of dead plants nearby. So, the worm poops and keeps moving. The worm will eat much more today.

Did You Know?
Worms can eat up to half of their body weight in a day.

CHAPTER 2

How They Decompose

In **ecosystems**, producers create their own food. Consumers eat other life-forms. And decomposers help break down dead material. Many worms are decomposers.

 Just 1 acre (0.4 ha) of soil can have millions of earthworms.

▶ **Worms often eat dead leaves.**

Earthworms are a common kind of worm. They live in soil. They open their mouths and eat the dirt around them. The soil includes **minerals**. It also includes dead material. Dead material often has a substance called cellulose. Other living things may eat cellulose. But their bodies can't break it down. Worms' bodies can.

When a worm swallows, the soil first reaches the worm's crop. This organ stores the soil. Then the soil moves into other organs. In the gizzard, small stones grind up the soil. After that, the soil moves into the intestine. That's where cellulose gets broken down.

> Some earthworms can be several feet long. Others are shorter than an inch.

Some of the soil's **nutrients** go into the worm's bloodstream. That is how the worm gets energy. The nutrients help the worm function. The rest of the soil comes out when the worm poops. Worm poop is called castings. The soil returns to the ground in a different form.

Thousands of kinds of worms exist. They decompose material all over the world. Worms do best in places with soil and moisture. Many live in warm woodlands and grasslands.

Did You Know?
Worms don't have teeth. That means worms can't chew their food. Instead, food gets broken up in their guts.

CHAPTER 3
Helping the Ecosystem

Worms eat soil to survive. But breaking down dead plants helps other living things, too. In fact, it helps the entire ecosystem. Without decomposers, dead material would start piling up.

 Earthworms can help gardens grow.

Decomposing does not take material away. Instead, it recycles the material. Worm poop contains many nutrients. Castings return these nutrients to the soil. For example, soil gains more nitrogen and phosphorus. These minerals make the soil richer.

Worms also help soil in other ways. As worms move and eat, they mix layers of soil. They also create tunnels. These actions make space for plant roots. Other useful

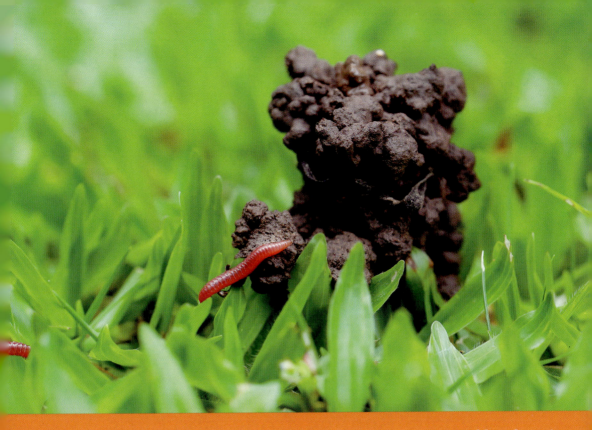

Most of the nitrogen in worms' food gets passed back out in their poop.

material can reach roots, too. For instance, water and oxygen can go deeper into the soil.

Good soil benefits the whole food chain. First, plants can grow better.

Then, plant-eating animals such as rabbits have more to eat. So, these animals increase in number. As a result, **predators** that eat rabbits can find more food.

Worms are also prey for many animals. Beetles, frogs, and birds all eat worms. Worms help other

Did You Know?
Scientists use worms to check soil health. If the soil is full of worms, the area is more likely to be healthy.

Birds may feed earthworms to their babies.

decomposers, too. For example, fungi and bacteria eat castings. Areas with many worms have more fungi and bacteria.

THAT'S AMAZING!

Worms and Water

Earthworms often go above ground when it rains. But other kinds of worms live underwater. Some types live in freezing Antarctic waters. Others live in hot springs. These worms have **adaptations** to live in harsh places.

Worms decompose underwater, too. They eat **sediment**. This process is similar to how earthworms eat soil on land. The underwater worms recycle the material. Their eating makes air pockets, too. That helps underwater plants grow. Just like on land, underwater worms help ecosystems.

Underwater worms help make water cleaner.

CHAPTER 4

Worm Danger

Worms help ecosystems. But they sometimes cause problems. They are **invasive** in certain places. One example is the northern forests of North America. Earthworms are not native to this area.

Night crawlers are common in North America. But they originally came from Western Europe.

By the 1800s, people brought earthworms to those forests. Many settlers had brought plants with them. Worms lived in the plants' soil. The worms began to eat and decompose in the new area. That has caused big changes to the soil.

In past years, certain plants had grown well in that soil. But now, native plants are facing trouble. For example, some earthworms hurt sugar maples. These trees grow better with more dead leaves

Today, people may accidentally bring invasive worms to new areas through fishing bait.

around. So do smaller plants. But earthworms eat the leaves. As a result, fewer small plants can grow in the area. Then animals such as deer have less food. They may eat young sugar maples instead.

Worms can harm native animals, too. Some birds and salamanders need the leaf litter. Without it, their numbers drop.

Climate change could bring more problems. Warmer weather can make ecosystems drier. Worms can't decompose as well in hot and

Did You Know?
Many worms are native to Canada. But today, three times more non-native worms live there.

> Worms need moisture to breathe. So, they can't survive long in dry areas.

dry areas. Warmer temperatures may also bring worms to different areas. For example, some places with frozen soil are heating up. If worms move to those areas, they may change more ecosystems.

Focus Questions

Write your answers on a separate piece of paper.

1. Write a few sentences explaining how worms help the ecosystem.

2. Would you want to have worms living near you? Why or why not?

3. What organ in a worm does soil reach first?
- **A.** the intestine
- **B.** the crop
- **C.** the gizzard

4. How could dead plant material protect sugar maple trees?
- **A.** It helps grow small plants for animals to eat instead of trees.
- **B.** It helps make trees stronger than any animal.
- **C.** It stops sugar maple trees from growing at all.

5. What does **benefits** mean in this book?

*Good soil **benefits** the whole food chain. First, plants can grow better. Then, plant-eating animals such as rabbits have more to eat.*

- **A.** helps something
- **B.** hurts something
- **C.** eats something

6. What does **prey** mean in this book?

*Worms are also **prey** for many animals. Beetles, frogs, and birds all eat worms.*

- **A.** animals that eat plants
- **B.** animals that get eaten
- **C.** animals that do not eat

Answer key on page 32.

Glossary

adaptations
Changes in an animal that make it better suited to its environment.

climate change
A human-caused global crisis involving long-term changes in Earth's temperature and weather patterns.

contracts
Brings a muscle together and makes it shorter.

ecosystems
The collections of living things in different natural areas.

invasive
Brought to a new place and spreading in a way that harms people, native plants, or native animals.

minerals
Substances that form naturally under the ground.

nutrients
Substances that living things need to stay strong and healthy.

predators
Animals that hunt other animals for food.

sediment
Stones, sand, or other materials that are carried by flowing water, wind, or ice.

To Learn More

BOOKS

Anderhagen, Anna. *Chasing the Mongolian Death Worm*. Minneapolis: Abdo Publishing, 2024.

Owen, Ruth. *Earth's Insects Need You!: Understand the Problems, How You Can Help, Take Action*. Minneapolis: Lerner Publications, 2024.

Rea, Amy C. *Soil*. Minneapolis: Abdo Publishing, 2020.

NOTE TO EDUCATORS

Visit **www.focusreaders.com** to find lesson plans, activities, links, and other resources related to this title.

Index

A
adaptations, 20

B
bacteria, 19

C
castings, 12–13, 16, 19
cellulose, 11
climate change, 26–27
consumers, 9

D
decomposers, 9, 15, 18–19

E
ecosystems, 9, 15, 20, 23, 26–27

F
food chain, 17–18
fungi, 19

I
invasive worms, 23–26

M
minerals, 10, 16

N
nutrients, 12, 16

O
organs, 11

P
predators, 18
producers, 9

S
sediment, 20

U
underwater worms, 20